GENERATING
BIG
ADVERTISING
IDEAS

3 ACTION FORMULA FOR *LOCAL* SMALL BUSINESS OWNERS & MANAGERS

DEREK JOHN PATTERSON

Copyright © 2018 Derek Patterson

All rights reserved. This book or any portion thereof may not be reproduced or used in any manner whatsoever without the express written permission of the publisher except for the use of brief quotations in a book review.

Printed in the United States of America

First Printing, 2018

ISBN-13: 978-1727253269

Derek Patterson Marketing
18 Arbor Drive, SSM, ON, P6C5L6

Table of Contents

Generating BIG Advertising IDEAS: 3 ACTION FORMULA 1

    Concept 1

    My 3 Favourite (and Most Productive) Brainstorming Techniques 2

    Here are 7 Common Scenarios where *you, as the leader,* may personally benefit from having a Brainstorming session: 3

    Here are 2 common scenarios where *you, as the Small Business Marketer*, may benefit from having a Brainstorming session: 4

    Here's why My 3 Favourite Brainstorming Techniques work…. 5

    Rules for Brainstorming Success 6

    Rule Breaker! Where I differ from the traditional rules of Brainstorming. 8

    My 3 Favourite (and Most Productive) Brainstorming Techniques. 10

    Getting Started (You don't need much to start with.) 10

    Favourite Brainstorming Technique #1 12

    Favourite Brainstorming Technique #2 17

    Favourite Brainstorming Technique #3 18

Generating BIG Advertising IDEAS Catalogue: For Local Small Business Owners & Managers 21

    Awesome Sales Event Themes 21

    Product Category Specific: IDEAS 29

    Christmas 35

    Ensuring an Effective Ad: Your Pre-Advertising Worksheet 39

    #1 Tip for Writing Ads. 44

Generating **BIG** Advertising **IDEAS**:
3 ACTION FORMULA

Concept

People say I'm creative and that I come up with good ideas. They say I 'make it look easy'! BIG Ideas are sparked with a little Solo Brainstorming session and I'm going to show you how to go about it.

The idea behind the Generating BIG Advertising IDEAS Catalogue is to equip small business owners with a secret weapon – your very own directory of novel advertising and sales promotional ideas that you could easily access whenever you need to plan a new campaign. Tons of ideas are already started for you. That's huge, in itself.

My 3 Favourite (and Most Productive) Brainstorming Techniques will help you improve your creative skills. You will learn new ways to easily generate brand new, original ideas from scratch. With these insights, you'll become an idea generating machine ☺. People will be saying that *you* make it look easy! I really want you to have this advantage.

Sure, you can find tons of Brainstorming info online. 2 of these techniques are commonly known and easily found. I'll show you how I've used them hundreds of times to come up with ideas that make business sense and get results. Then there's a 3rd technique that I'm sure isn't rocket science, I just haven't heard anyone promoting it before.

After completing your Pre-Advertising Worksheet, you will forever create successful, effective commercials.

This is basically a questionnaire. Once you really absorb all your answers, you'll never have to worry about having bad, meaningless ads again and you'll never waste another dollar on media ad packages that don't fit.

All in all, you have 3 new tools in your toolkit that will help you become a better, wiser marketer. Your business will thrive on new ideas. You are on the path to a sales increase and a larger piece of the pie. This can begin on your very next ad campaign.

If your sales growth has to cut into the profits of the Giants in your market (big name companies, Big Box, out-of-town spending and online shopping), then all the better. I live for helping local businesses rise up to the challenge and win!

My 3 Favourite (and Most Productive) Brainstorming Techniques

Brainstorming is commonly known as a group activity. However, as managers and leaders, it's often up to us to come up with winning ideas and strategies that will hit the numbers. Sure, we need great teams and great people to succeed but not every initiative is going to be the result of a democratic decision. Nor do we always have time to ask for everyone's ideas. There are going to be times when we simply need to do it ourselves, ASAP. Being able to create profitable ideas while executing with efficiency are critical survival skills.

You can do this even if you feel you are 'not creative'.

I hear so many people say, 'I'm not creative', 'I don't know what to do', 'I need new ideas', 'you're the expert' or 'I'm too busy to think about that right now'. Then what happens? They end up delaying their planning. They end up running the same old ho-hum routine ads because they are up against their deadlines. Customers and clients don't see anything more special about you than the next company. 'They're all the same', they say.

It's no wonder why so many small business owners and managers dread advertising and feel their advertising budget is a total waste of money.

Can creating ads become a more enjoyable experience rather than a 'necessary evil'? Can your business grow because you've spiced up your marketing plan with new themes? I hope so. After all, this is advertising! It's supposed to be fun!

Creativity will easily come to you when you find a Brainstorming system that works for you.

Here are 7 Common Scenarios where *you, as the leader,* may personally benefit from having a Brainstorming session:

1. You have a problem to solve and don't have all the time in the world to solve it.

2. You have a huge goal to hit and you *know* it's going to require 'new and different' strategies if you are ever going to achieve it.

3. There's a big, comprehensive project coming up.

4. You want your team involved, engaged and working towards common goals.

5. You want to improve yours and/or your team's creative thinking levels.

6. You have a project or initiative that needs a 'fresh coat of paint', so to speak.

7. You are overwhelmed.

Let's take a moment to discuss 'overwhelm' because some of you may really feel this way. Brainstorming is my saviour when I'm overwhelmed and I'm feeling the pressure to perform.

Here's the scenario. There are times when you have to step up and hit one out of the park. Yet, you have two strikes against you because you're feeling the weight of a seemingly insurmountable to-do list. Meetings, employees, customers, firefighting ...all have you racing on your hamster wheel.

You aren't just running on the hamster wheel, you're juggling, dodging and ducking at the same time.

Now, to have to dream up a plan from scratch...make it great... and ensure it makes business sense within the allotted time-frame and budget...well, this can be tough to get going on. Nerve-wracking, too!

No pressure though. *'We've got this'*.

<u>At the beginning, all we want you to do is get thoughts on paper.</u>

Here are 2 common scenarios where *you, as the Small Business Marketer*, may benefit from having a Brainstorming session:

1. **When we need to create themes and impactful messaging for Ad Campaigns, Sales Promotions or Events by being different, meaningful and relevant.**

The Brainstorming session starts with figuring out what we want to say to the audience. Then the theme falls into place. You see, for any message or theme to work, it *must* resonate with your target market. Once your message reaches the eyes and ears of your primary customer or client, we want them to instantly say 'this is for me'. Once they are tuned in, we have the opportunity to say something meaningful enough to move them towards whatever action you want them to take. Only when we get their attention can we expect them to hear our offer.

We must invest our efforts in determining what works for the customer, not what works for us. Often, this requires some Brainstorming to hash things out because we have to break through our natural instinct to think of our goals first.

2. **When there's a humungous Sales Promotion to plan.**

Because of their importance to the company, some events are in a category of their own. They receive a significant ad budget. A huge, community-wide impact may be necessary to hit ambitious revenue targets. They are harder to manage because there are so many moving parts, so many more staff and suppliers are involved, and so much has to go smoothly. Not only do you need the BIG Idea, but there's also so much more planning to think through. Results are a must.

Besides generating a brilliant and awesome idea, Brainstorming will help you present an organized, thoughtful plan to your team.

Here's why My 3 Favourite Brainstorming Techniques work….

- ✓ They allow the mind to flow freely.
- ✓ They open up the box so I can climb out.
- ✓ My most pressing problems are often resolved within minutes.
- ✓ They allow me to tap into the deepest recesses of my mind, where the great ideas and best solutions are waiting to be discovered.
- ✓ Ideas bounce around, making new connections. One idea leads to another. Ideas evolve and take a life of their own. Next thing you know, there's that 'Eureka!' or 'AHA!' moment that gives you goosebumps.
- ✓ They allow me to break free and be creative and productive even when I don't feel like it! It's sometimes not easy to get motivated to sit down and make a serious plan when one is already overwhelmed from day-to-day life.
- ✓ Ultimately, using these Brainstorming techniques helps create better advertising campaigns for my small business clients so they can make more money…and that's what I want for you!

Rules for Brainstorming Success

- Write your Objective down. (Don't just keep it in the back of your mind).
- Start with the belief that all things are possible. Have a 'how can we do it?' attitude.
- Disregard the rules that pop into your head.
- Don't judge your thoughts. Judgement is out. Free thinking is in.
- Always remember, we are looking for ways to improve our current situation. We want something better than what we currently have.
- Use pen/pencil and scrap paper...do not use a device. (When you are using your hand to write, you are triggering a neuro-motor physical activity...your brain is lighting up!)
- Set aside 15-30 minutes. Since our mind likes to work in short bursts, 15 minutes is optimal. If you can, don't book anything else for 30 minutes because if you get into a 'flow state', you won't want to stop.
- We are going for quantity. Let's get as much on paper as possible. (With exception. I'll talk more about this when we talk about the Flow State.)
- If time permits, 'sleep on it' and schedule a follow-up session the next day.
- Give yourself permission to jot down everything that comes to mind, even if it's a problem or an unrelated thought. Yes, I encourage bringing up potential problems. Yes, this may throw you off course but if you have problems lingering in the back of your mind, they will prevent you from getting to the best ideas. Here's why that is...

If you ignore or force a thought away, the thought will remain just under the surface. An invisible barrier is formed that blocks you from accessing deeper thinking. It's like a 'Do Not Enter' sign.

This seems to be the way nature works. Have you ever found that if you push a thought or a problem away it actually sticks more and keeps coming back? This is because you are subconsciously telling your mind that there's something it must pay attention to, for your own protection. You have to acknowledge the problems in order to free your mind.

That's the beauty of Brainstorming. It gives us permission to think and write down anything that comes to mind. This includes negative thoughts.

If you believe, like I do, that problems create opportunities, your next genius idea *could* originate from one of your toughest challenges. You just never know.

And hey, if problem-solving takes up your Brainstorming session time, try not to feel like it's a big loss. Dealing with these issues has to be done sooner or later. You can always re-schedule another session and go into it with a better chance to come up with something amazing.

Why 'I'm going to sleep on it' really does work.

Why do my best ideas come while I'm in the car? On the way home? Or in the middle of the night?

Why is it that I can have a 'great meeting' with a client or co-worker but still have the best ideas come to me later?

The answer? It's because our mind is working while at rest.

When we are resting or doing mindless tasks, our thoughts freely bounce back and forth like the ball in a pinball machine. Options open up. Your chances at finding a new, workable solution improve.

You see, our brains are the greatest information processors and problem-solving machines ever created. They do their best work when they are at rest. Information is processed. Trash is sifted through. Clarity is left behind.

A fresh mind will explore new ideas. A full mind will take the path of least resistance (which ends up being the same old, same old).

We can't always 'sleep on it' though.

Having said that, I acknowledge that we don't always have time to wait. If we waited for a fresh mind, we may never get any business done! However, there are a couple things we can do to help ourselves when under a time crunch; 1) realize at what time of day we are the freshest and to schedule our thinking time accordingly and 2) try to have a buffer between the end of your brainstorming session and the time you have to make a final decision.

Even if you believe you have the best idea ever – it's still nice to give yourself time to let it sink in. If it's a great idea, it will still be a great idea in the morning. Having said that, what if it's *not* really a great idea after all? You'll be happy you didn't bark up the wrong tree. A lost day now is better than weeks of struggles.

Another benefit of 'sleeping on it' is that it allows us time to consult with a trusted co-worker.

Whether I've Brainstormed with a client, co-worker or by myself, I'll find a confidante to talk the idea(s) out with. With almost certainty, they'll offer a new perspective. Fresh eyes may spy pitfalls that weren't obvious right away. Also, it really is fun and exciting to bounce ideas back and forth with someone you love working with.

Thirdly, and I love this one, you can test-run ideas simply by talking them out loud. Sometimes, you don't need anyone to say anything. Clarity comes simply from hearing your own voice.

In summary, sleep on it! If you can. Give the best ideas a chance to marinate in your mind. If you had a great idea, it will only get better. If your idea wasn't so great after all, you've saved yourself a lot of grief. If you have an opportunity to talk things through with someone, go for it.

Rule Breaker! Where I differ from the traditional rules of Brainstorming.

The #1 rule of Brainstorming is to go for quantity; to write out as many ideas as possible. You aren't supposed to go too deep on any one idea. You can quickly capture many ideas by jotting down one or two keywords.

For the sake of speed, you are only permitted to apply logic and practicality after your session is up. You aren't supposed to spend too much time on one thought.

However, there is an exception in my books.

The idea is still to go for quantity, but when something feels right, like an 'AHA!' moment, I'll stop and expand on it. I don't wait to come back to it later.

I'll add more creative ideas. I'll include any questions or challenges that surface. If any 'next steps' come to mind, they get jotted down. Anything and everything goes on paper. Wherever my mind wants to go, it ends up on paper.

I'll go deeper by asking more specific questions. I'll take advantage of the mood and take this idea as far as I can.

- Who needs to be involved?

- What resources might I need?
- When?
- How can I make this idea even better?

A plan takes shape. An action list forms. Progress!

At this point, you're in a **Flow State.** Your brain is firing on all cylinders. You are so focused. You are feeling creative and brilliant. Everything is coming to you easily.

When you are in a Flow State, you DO NOT want to lose it. It's a gift. It's so hard to get there sometimes. Capitalizing here and now is really important.

You could end up with your project half mapped out without really trying!

Once you've taken your AHA idea as far as you can, it's time to switch back to brainstorming for quantity. Take another peek at the Objective and start writing. You'll still want as many options available to you as possible. And, hey, maybe the next idea is *the* BIG idea.

Let's flow right into…

My 3 Favourite (and Most Productive) Brainstorming Techniques.

Before we begin, I would like you to feel confident in knowing...

- You are creative, even if you think you're not. Even when you have a hard time mustering up the energy for it.
- You'll solve problems more quickly and more easily than ever before.
- You can up your game when it comes to creating fresh, new & different advertising campaigns.

Getting Started (You don't need much to start with.)

a) Paper and something to write with.
b) 15-30 minutes.
c) Close your door. Turn off your email notifications. Silence your phone.
d) Set an Objective. You need to get from Point A to Point B. Point A is where you are now. Point B is your Objective, in other words, where you want to go.
e) Edit your Objective down to a few words. 1 word would be ideal but having a short phrase is fine.
f) Define where you are now. Write it out so you have clarity on where you are now.
g) Start writing what comes to mind.

Point A. Where are you now?

_____
_____
_____
_____
_____

Point B. Your Objective. What outcome do you want to see?

_____
_____
_____
_____
_____

Redefine the Objective. Let's polish it and write it on your Brainstorming page.

_____

Favourite Brainstorming Technique #1

Mind Mapping

Here's why I love Mind Mapping.

First and foremost, MM fires up the brain – even if it's tired. The switchboard lights up. Engagement comes rather quickly.

This must be because MM doesn't follow a strict format. You don't have an order to follow. It goes with how the mind works. You aren't creating bulleted lists. Ideas are allowed to bounce around. Information is allowed to flow freely. Associations form. Clusters of ideas develop.

Great ideas seem to come without too much effort.

Mind Mapping can help you to…

- See the big picture.
- Pull a wide range of thoughts together onto a single page.
- Connect thoughts and ideas together.
- Tap into new ways of thinking.
- Explore your options.
- Advance your project quickly.

What Mind Mapping is not…

- A linear way of thinking.
- Black and white.
- Rigid.
- Intimidating.

Getting started on Mind Mapping

1. Give yourself a time limit.

2. Grab the largest piece of paper possible. You want lots of room to get messy.

3. Center your Objective on the page and place a circle or a thought cloud around it.

4. Each new thought or idea radiates from your Objective, looking almost like a solar system. Circle the new thoughts and connect them to the Objective with a line, similar to branches on a tree.

5. Each new thought may trigger its own set of associated ideas. Ideas will spring from ideas. Connect them. You'll see sub-categories and themes develop.

Indeed, you'll end up with a page that resembles a solar system. Your Objective represents the sun. The ideas orbiting the Objective represent the planets. Several of the planets have their own associated ideas, or moons, orbiting around them.

(We can even change the name from Mind Mapping to Universal Thinking!)

6. Try to use keywords only. You want to work quickly. You are going for volume. You want to capture as many thoughts as possible, so choose words that will help you remember what you were thinking when you first wrote them down.

Mind Mapping a Major Project

Projects need structure. Directing a project takes special talents. There are so many moving parts, details, steps, deadlines, people...

By MM, you can execute a smooth running, successful program with proper planning, clear communication and accountability.

- ✓ You can assemble your project in one or two sessions.
- ✓ You can organize your project into manageable chunks.
- ✓ Action lists form.
- ✓ Timelines and deadlines are established.
- ✓ Budgets are developed (or followed).
- ✓ You can explain your strategy with clarity.
- ✓ You can clearly communicate what's expected from all interested parties.
- ✓ Contingency plans are already formed in the back of your mind. Inevitably, you'll run into situations. The good news is you have an inventory of alternative ideas from your first Brainstorming session. There were ideas you didn't use that now make perfect Plan B's. (Plus, you'll look like a genius when you pull solutions out of thin air!)

Mind Mapping in a Group Setting

The intention behind My 3 Favourite Brainstorming Techniques is to show you how to quickly generate fantastic and original ideas while solo brainstorming. Since Brainstorming sessions are usually held in group settings, I'd be remiss if I didn't share one particular (and maybe unusual) insight I have regarding *effective group Brainstorming*.

I'm referring to whole team participation. This means getting contributions from your Quiet Ones! There are those who don't say too much for a variety of reasons such as; fear of being criticized, second-guessing themselves, or they are simply wired to think things through before they speak.

What happens during a typical boardroom Brainstorming session? The outgoing folks take the spotlight. They openly speak their ideas. They feed off each other. They bounce ideas back and forth. They form the dynamics of a great Brainstorming meeting. This is what we want, after all. As managers, we are usually happy with this. However, we have to ask ourselves if we are reaching our potential when we haven't heard from the whole team.

When team members keep their ideas to themselves, your company loses because you miss out on thoughtful, intelligent, innovative ideas from people who can naturally see where all the pieces fit.

Our business culture seems to favour the outgoing and enthusiastic personalities. If we understand why some people take longer to express their ideas than others, we can come up with a solution to increase participation.

If you are dealing with introverts, you need to know they require time to reflect on all the information they heard. Asking for instant ideas might not yield anything. They'll go through a process of evaluating the Objective, they'll consider the pros and cons of all the ideas heard, make connections and draw conclusions. They'll see the big picture and respond accordingly. This takes time but you'll get good answers and brilliant, thoughtful ideas!

My suggestion is to make your Mind Mapping/Brainstorming Session a two-part session.

The beauty of having the Second Session.

MM is a visual tool that makes insecure people feel comfortable because there's truly no such thing as a bad idea. Every idea connects somewhere. It could connect to the Objective. It could line up to a cluster of ideas already started. There's a place for every idea no matter how crazy or vanilla it seems or how unsure the volunteer may feel. No one has to keep their ideas to themselves. If they do...this is where the second session pays off.

You see, by offering a follow-up session, you are allowing extra thinking time. This benefits the entire staff, not only the thinkers in the group.

Everyone has the day to submit their ideas or they bring their ideas to the next day's meeting. Also, emails and 'do you have a second?' meetings are allowed throughout the day.

You have now offered your entire staff several ways to contribute. You've accommodated several preferred communications styles and have done all you can to generate as many ideas as possible.

Here's how your 2 MM sessions could be structured:

Session One - a wide open session.

- Explain the Objective to your team. Explain what you want to achieve and why it's very important to everyone.
- Take the pressure off everyone by letting them know it's okay if nothing comes to them during the meeting. There will be time after the meeting for new ideas.
- You would like as many ideas as possible.
- All ideas and associations are to be written down.
- Make it clear that all ideas are welcome. There are no bad ideas.
- There's absolutely no criticism allowed.
- *'We did that before and it didn't work'* is also not allowed.

Session Two – new ideas and narrowing things down.

- The MM has been cleaned up and organized. 'Here's where we left off.'
- Session 1 ideas are clustered into themes or groups.
- Add any new ideas.
- Prioritize themes according to their fit against the Objective.
- Discussion time – an opportunity to expand on anything on the board.
- Choose the Top 2 or 3 concepts for further discussion, unless of course, your team has already been running with the BIG idea.
- Discuss Next Steps.
- Create the Action Plan.

Favourite Brainstorming Technique #2

The Word Storm

It's similar to Mind Mapping but without the map. You simply write one-word ideas, blindly and freely until your time is up. All you are doing is dumping every thought you have, as it relates to advertising, onto a piece of paper.

Step 1. Find 15 minutes of 'alone time'. (Set aside 30 minutes just in case you are in a groove.)

Step 2. Visualize your Objective and start writing one-word ideas like crazy. If you can't do it in one word, so be it. Don't force yourself to follow rules to a tee. Write everything down. Get it all out of your mind and onto that paper.

Step 3. It's evaluation time. Go back over your words and phrases and see what grabs you and makes the most business sense.

Step 4. Narrow your options down according to best fits against the Objective.

Step 5. Expand on the best ideas.

Step 6. Optional idea: get clarity simply by sharing your best ideas out loud to a friend.

Next Step? It depends. There really isn't an official next step. Possibly, you…

- Have found your 'aha' moment through this exercise.
- See other problems that need to be solved as part of your overall solution.
- Need to consult others before you can proceed.
- Need to sleep on it some more.

Either way, you've made significant progress. Congratulations.

Favourite Brainstorming Technique #3

Rewrite ~ Repurpose ~ Research: Ad Copy Starters

This is a great little technique for small business owners who are on a mission to find the right words for their ads and promotions.

Sometimes, all it takes is for a single word or a phrase to appear and it triggers the BIG Idea.

Here's how I go about it. It's an online search. I have an idea of what I want to get across but don't know the best way to say it. I'm looking for those words that motivate me. (No plagiarizing is allowed, of course.)

I conduct the Search. Page 1 of Results opens up. Each result contains 3 parts: 1) a headline, 2) a one or two-sentence description and 3) the web address.

I scan the headlines and the descriptions. I can go through several pages within minutes.

I have 3 criteria in mind as I'm scanning:

1. Phrasing that speaks my customer's language…something that would match the conversation that's going on in their heads.
2. Phrasing that would nicely portray my client's business/service/product in the eyes of the customer.
3. Ways to come across as authentic and of service. No meaningless clichés are allowed.

We want the words that make your audience say to themselves 'this is for me' within moments of seeing or hearing your advertisement. If we can get this reaction, we've increased the chances that the rest of the ad will be caught and the desired action will be taken.

Allow me to explain why this strategy generates good copy ideas. You see, the copy for a website should be written for SEO (Search Engine Optimization). This means they strategically use the words and the phrases that they know shoppers are using when searching. Therefore, if we use similar wording in our communications, we are speaking our customer's language. Our messages become meaningful and relevant. They work.

Taking the research effort one step further, I'll click through to review the websites that caught my attention. Sometimes more great lines fall right into my lap. With a little rewriting, ta-da! We've cooked up a message that has good odds to get great results.

Here's a Search Tip:

Try not to overthink your search terms. I used to find myself trying to figure out the exact wording that would surely generate many results. I began seeing better results when I simply typed the phrase or words that were on my mind. I gave up on trying to engineer the perfect wording. I want to find the closest fit to what I have in mind, not necessarily the most results.

Here's an experiment I did while I was writing this section of the book. I'd like to report the results to you.

I acted as if I was researching for a Clothing Store. The objective is to find new promotional ideas and new copy ideas for the fall marketing plan. The target market is professional women.

It's natural to start with a wide search term such as *'advertising promotions for clothing stores'*. The results page shows many store promotions. I'm reminded that it's rare for me to find anything unique when the market is heavy with Big Box stores and the Franchises. They aren't often doing anything too creative or thoughtful. They want to push the deal. Their advertising copy is usually light on the authentic wording that I'm looking for. I end up with little to work with. (Often, the best content comes from astute small business owners.)

Next, I searched for something more specific...'business attire for professional women'. Two sentences instantly caught my attention because I knew they would catch my target market's attention.

1. *'Wondering what to wear to your next job interview or your first day of work?'*
2. *'Professional business attire should convey your credibility and competence, but also reflect some personality without going overboard'*.

My instant thoughts were...

Re: #1)

This is good. Targeting job interviewers is a little too narrow of a target market for my client but there's something to this headline. Everyone wonders what to wear to work whether it's their first day, a special day or any day for that matter.

By specifically speaking with people who are going to job interviews or those who are on their 1st-day-on-the-job, it would suggest you will always look like today is a special day after you've shopped here.

-What is your interpretation?-

Re: #2)

I really like the educational, informative feel of this. The store employees are positioned as experts right away; without sounding cliché. If you want advice and a personal touch when shopping for professional business attire, it's here. They don't have to say 'we're experts'. <u>*Their expert status comes across by clearly knowing what's important to the target market.*</u>

To top it off, the wording is so relevant. Who doesn't want to look credible, competent and with a suitable amount of personality? This really is great copy.

-What do you think?-

The moral of the story is 2 great ad copy starters presented themselves within seconds. Each had a vastly different position.

Try it for yourself. You will come up with NEW ideas. Your messaging will be much more effective than most of your competitors, big or small. You may be able to relate to your customers/clients/patients so well that they would never consider giving anyone else their business.

It took me longer to type this exercise than to come up with a couple of great ideas.

On so many occasions, I've heard small local business owners tell me 'I don't know what to say'. Well, here's an easy place to start. Just look for the right words in a simple online search and let an idea or two come to you.

Before you go, I would like to make you an offer. If you want to Brainstorm ideas for your next ad campaign, please consider my 1:1 IDEAS Session. This is a 45-minute coaching call over the phone or skype. We'll work together to find your next BIG Idea.

Simply flip me an email with a couple lines that cover what you are hoping to achieve and I'll reply with my offer, along with appointment suggestions.

'Let's get some good ideas going.'

Derek

derekpatterson@shaw.ca

Generating **BIG** Advertising **IDEAS** Catalogue: For Local Small Business Owners & Managers

180 Inventive and Imaginative Revenue Generating Concepts.

'A personal resource for Small Business Marketers who need new inspirations for your next ad campaign, sales promotion, or event'.

Awesome Sales Event Themes

Save Your Receipts. Today Could Be Your Lucky Discount Day- At the end of the month, throw a dart at the calendar. Where the dart lands, that's the Lucky Day where all customers who show receipts from this date can return to the store for a 50% cash rebate or store credit. This is an alternative to the typical '50% off Storewide Sale'. Post the Lucky Day on your social media channels. Consider taking the opportunity to announce the promotion is being repeated again this month. Customers may start to follow your social media so they get messaged instantly whenever a Lucky Discount Day is announced.

Make Your Own Sale- Contest winners are allowed to choose their own sale item up to a certain $ amount. Pre-determine a specific number of contest winners. Consider having a random draw for a grand prize so all customers feel they have a shot at winning something big.

Alternatively, pick a time where everyone can select an item for 50% off (with restrictions, of course. For example, any product under $30 can be had at 50% off).

Boss is Away- The employees are hosting a massive sale while the boss is away.

Bad Luck Clearance- Friday the 13th. *'The store had bad luck. Some merchandise has been on shelves for far too long. This is good luck for bargain hunters on Friday the 13th...'* As an added touch, give away a good luck charm with every purchase.

Brainstorming Notes.

_____
_____
_____
_____

No Profit Clearance Sale- A $100 reward is offered if items are not sold exactly at cost. Let the public know the reason for the sale is to make room for new season merchandise.

Cashback Days- Offer $1 cash back for every $10 spent. *'10% is rebated back to you.'* This could be offered as a cash rebate or a gift card. The gift card ensures a return visit to the store.

Inventory Pile-Up Sale- Display your *'pile of values'*. Quantities of merchandise are priced to sell at low prices. Inventory is in a pile or stacked in a certain section of the store.

White Elephant Sale- *'You'll find 'White Elephant' merchandise in every department. Nice merchandise that no one is talking about. Enjoy peanut sized prices on jumbo values!'*

Balloon Sale- A classic. Include discounts inside the balloons. Everyone loves to pop balloons.

New Broom Sale- Explain that *'you want to sweep your shelves clean of old inventory.'* Offer free brooms for buying quantity or certain items. Dress employees as janitors or cleaners. Invite customers to come *'clean-up'*.

Over Parked Inventory Sale- Your ads are designed to look like a Summons. *'Come bail out overstocked, over parked goods.'* Mark your discounts with look-a-like parking tickets. Offer greater discounts on second offenders or goods that are on sale for a second time.

It's A Record Day- Let it be known you want to set records. Items are marked down to their lowest prices of the year. Have door crashers. Publicly post sales records you plan to surpass.

Money Horn- The 'money horn' blows throughout the day. Customers standing at the cash register at the same time the horn blows, receive a bonus discount or freebie.

One Dollar Sale- Buy the 2nd item for a dollar (or a penny). *'A dollar never bought so much'*. This sounds more interesting than a Buy 1 Get 1 Free. Another slogan could be *'Bring a friend. Their purchase is only a dollar.'*

Mad Butcher- Dress up as a butcher because you are *'wheeling and dealing and chopping prices'*.

Floor to Ceiling- Discounts on everything for the house...paint, carpet, flooring, etc. This could turn into a contest to win a free Room Make-over.

Brainstorming Notes.

_____
_____
_____
_____
_____

Cause 10 Sale- This is an ideal way to extend a sale. You haven't sold all the inventory you need to so you are having a Cause 10 Sale. *'Why a Cause 10 sale? Cause there's only 10 left.'* Create demand and scarcity by having only limited quantities available.

Community Garage Sale- Host a massive garage sale. Invite the public to book a table to sell their own goods. Charge a registration fee. The fee goes to charity.

No Sale Theme- Not sure what kind of promotion to do this month? Consider promoting this: *'We don't have a special sale this month so we're just going to say thank you to our customers with an X discount. We're pleased to be your store for….'*

Random Sales Themes…Rainy Day Specials, Sunshine Sales, Snowfall Steals, Foggy Day Discounts, Seniors Week, Coming Out of the Cold Sale Event, Specials Aren't the Only Thing You'll Find at….

Peanuts Party- Great sale prices. *'Pay peanuts.'* Offer customers peanuts to snack on.

Monster Sale- The staff dresses up. This event can be held anytime *'the sales are monster'*. Monster Sales don't have to be limited to October.

Midnight Sales- Off-hour events always attract a lot of attention because they are so unusual.

6AM Sales or Early Bird Sales- Open early and offer breakfast.

Winter Warmth Sale- Sunny Values. Tag merchandise with 'Red Hot Values' and 'Sunny Values'. Offer free blankets or hold a draw for a super warm coat. If you have enough mark-up, you could go as far as offering a tropical vacation as a grand prize. Or, simply go with gloves, cool scarves, hats, mitts, etc. with every purchase…whatever it takes to strengthen the 'warmth' message.

Clean Sweep Sale- *'Come sweep up the savings.'* Dramatize the event by giving away free brooms.

Storewide White Sale- Everything white is on sale. For example; clothing, bakery, autos, appliances, grocery. (If White Sales are already being used in your market, especially in January, pick another colour and hold a better sale.)

Brainstorming Notes.

_____
_____
_____
_____
_____

T-Shirt Tuesday- Boost a slower sales day. Offer a free company or sports team t-shirt with $100 or more spent.

Pre-Sale or Preview Party- Pre-Sale invitations are sent prior to the sale date. Crank up the demand by offering a *'limited number'* of invites.

New Product Launch- This is an invitation that appeals to early adopters. *'You're invited to come try it out before anyone else.'*

Restaurants/International Foods Ad Copy Idea- *'Come to Italy. Don't go to Italy, let Italy come to you.'*

Over Stocked Inventory Sale Ad Copy Idea- *'We simply have too much stock on hand. We must clean out our inventory.'* Honesty works in advertising.

The UFO Event Ad Copy Idea- *'UFO's have been sighted! Unearth Fabulous Offers!'*

The Paranormal Sales Event Ad Copy Idea- 'Enjoy unexpected savings'.

Loading Dock Sale- The loading docks are stocked with inventory. Sell inventory straight from the truck or the docks because you don't want to haul it in. *'We're saving on labour and transferring the savings to you.'*

Outside Sale Event Ad Copy Idea- *'Because there's not enough room to get it all inside, merchandise is stranded outside. It's all Quick Sale priced.'*

Passing the Buck- Each customer who comes in through the week receives a numbered card. Invite them to come back on Saturday to see if their number matches yours. If they have a match, they win. If they have a match by 10am, they win $100. If the money is not claimed, the buck gets passed and the next number is drawn. The prize is now reduced to $75 if the winner comes by noon. You can keep up the same idea going until the prize works its way down to $20.

Beat the Heat- Sale prices on 'cool products'. Consider giveaways of related products such as a free frosty mug to the first 90 customers or pick a number that matches today's forecast.

Back *from* School Sale- Promote summer fun items when the kids are back home from school and the parents are eager to get them out of the house.

Brainstorming Notes.

_____
_____
_____
_____
_____

Ad Copy Idea for The *We're Looking for an Excuse to Have a Sale* Sale- *'This week only. We'll find an excuse to offer you a deal on anything you want in the store'.*

Low Price Guarantee- Offer a refund plus 10% more if a lower price is found in your store within 60 days. (This may stand out more because 30 days is the standard policy).

Half of the Store is Half Price for Half a Day- Draw a line down the middle of the store and declare one side is 'half off' for the afternoon.

Baby Boomer Video Game Challenge- use Asteroids, Space Invaders and Pac Man for the contest. This retro contest is sure to generate a lot of buzz with your 40+ crowd.

Get It Together! - This is a good promo for products that have a sister product, such as appliances. Buy a washer/dryer, fridge/stove, receive a nice discount on the second item.

By the Pound- Price by the pound like grocery stores do. Furniture, appliances, cars, etc. Create a smart slogan like *'Our fridges cost less per pound than the steak you'll put in them.'*

Friday the 13th- Customers submit their horror stories to win a collection of horror movies.

Furniture of Your Dreams- *'If you had a $10,000 imaginary budget, how would you spend it?'* Customers submit their dream list. They browse the store to find their favourites. There may be a real pay-off here from word of mouth advertising when they tell their friends and family about an eye-catching piece they saw in your showroom. Ask if they would mind being called if any items go on sale. The contest winner gets one thing they want off their list.

Ugly Themes- *'Tired of the embarrassment?'* Send photos of your ugly carpet, bath, etc. to win a $2000 store credit or win a complete makeover.

Our Manager Has Gone Nuts- S/he marked everything down and left us a bag of peanuts behind! Update the pricing after 2 days because the manager's gone nuts again! (You could almost build a brand by doing silly promotions on a regular basis. Customers will pay attention to see what you are going to come up with next!)

Free Digital Cameras with Purchase- This is an affordable and nice gift. There are endless photo-related promotional ideas.

Silent Auction Ad Copy Idea- *'We can't keep quiet about it. You have to be here.'*

<u>Brainstorming Notes.</u>

_____
_____
_____
_____
_____

Top Secret Sale- Prices are not displayed in your advertising because the tags are blacked out. Prices are bleeped out of audio ads. Customers must go to the store to see the prices. Your ad copy explains that you *'don't want to advertise prices because you don't want to add to our competitor's misery. Nobody would believe these prices are so low.'* Add a real touch by blacking out your store windows.

Hottest Ticket in Town- Free Passes/Tickets. Offer free passes or tickets with purchase. When you have tickets to sold-out events, you are holding a pair of the Hottest Tickets in Town!

Slogan Search- Invite your customers to help you come up with a new slogan. *'Bring in your XYZ Company slogan idea. If we use it in our ads, you win a…'*

Yard Sale- Everyone loves a yard sale. If you have miscellaneous merchandise piled high and want to get rid of it fast and at a cheap price, go with the Yard Sale. If you have the room, you can grow the size of the event by allowing the public to set up their own tables.

Discover Our Store- Shoppers receive a card when they enter the store. 4 items are featured. When shoppers figure out which aisles the items are stocked in, they can enter for the random draw. Make it a Passport theme simply by positioning a stamp near select products. Either way, this is a clever strategy to get people circulating through large stores, malls, downtown districts, home shows, etc.

Losing Lottery Tickets- This is a good idea for a less commonly known lottery ticket outlet. Customers bring in losing lottery tickets in return for store discounts or additional draws. *'Bring in the losers, win with a discount.'*

Bank for a Day- Customers put money in your 'bank' and get more back. For example, they can deposit $100 and get $110 in merchandise. This sounds more fun and creative than the standard 10% off.

Blowout Sale Ad Copy Idea- 'We *have overly inflated inventory that has to be sold'*.

Shopping Cart Race- Have fun. Gather a crowd to cheer contestants through an obstacle course. Have heats similar to the Olympics. Fill carts with Paper Towels for the 1st Round. Work your way down to a final Shopping Cart Race Champion.

Brainstorming Notes.
_____
_____
_____
_____

Guess the Grocery Bill, Get the Grub- Fill a cart or basket with goods. Customers guess the value of the goods without going over.

Diamond Mine- Set up a sandpit and bury a diamond in it. Qualifiers get a plot or section to dig ...with a spoon.

Power Equipment Timing Contests- These ideas work for anything powered by a motor. For example; guess when the snow blower will run out of gas (or the car or a 4-wheeler or a lawn tractor). Another idea is to guess how long it will take for a lawn tractor to travel from point A to B.

Ten Pound Turkey with Purchase- A 10-day event leading up to Thanksgiving/Christmas. 10 is always a good number to use in marketing.

The Gigantic Jelly Bean Contest- Guess the number of jelly beans in the jar to win a surprisingly huge prize. Use the largest jar you can find. Using a big prize makes the basic jelly bean contest the talk of the town. Bigger is always better.

The Big Booty Treasure Chest- Have a pirate/treasure theme. Display (100) items to be won and one winner takes the entire booty.

'Chicken Out' Sale- Every customer gets a free meal from a partnering Chicken Restaurant.

Musician Match Game- Randomly post pics of artists along with their baby pics. Customers match them up to win.

Service with A Smile- The first 50 customers who enter the store with a smile receive a $10 gift card.

WE GOOFED UP!- Be totally honest and tell the public that you really goofed by buying way too much inventory. Now it has to be cleared out. *'We bought way too many! Now we have to clear them out at huge discounts!'*

We Have Buyer's Remorse Sale- Here's another promotion where you are guilty of buying too much inventory and now it has to go. *'We have Buyer's Remorse. Our buyers bought too much inventory and now we have to clear it at huge discounts! Take advantage of our Buyer's Remorse sale. You won't regret it!'*

<u>Brainstorming Notes.</u>

_____
_____
_____
_____
_____

Unlock It To Win It- This works for anything that requires a key or a code to open it. Have contestants take a crack at it. When it unlocks, you have a winner. This could be a car, house, or a safe...or even a bike lock.

Competitions- Generate some buzz when you host a customer challenge. Watch your word of mouth and social media take off. Ideas for **Food Eating Competitions** include Biggest Burgers, the Most Wings, Pizza, Hot Dogs, or Ice Cream (up for a Winter Ice Cream challenge?). How about a **Sandwich Building Contest**? **Board Game Competitions** can include Scrabble or Trivial Pursuit. Or go off the board with an idea like Rock Paper Scissors, Arm Wrestling or...Air Guitar!

OverHead UnderWear- This is silly but people will talk about it. Can we get 10 people to enter the store wearing underwear on their head for $50? Maybe this idea could tie in with the Drop Your Pants Sale theme?

Customer Testimonials- Testimonials offer social proof that you are a trusting business to deal with. Use a copy theme that goes along the lines of *'Straight from the people...testimonial...'*

Selfie Award- Your customers nominate themselves to win. Print the pics and post them on a store wall...not just online. Make customers visit the store. This will make for great conversation pieces. Customers will search for themselves and other people they know.

Messy Desk Contest- Nominate your co-worker who is notorious for their messy desk.

Shop Early...for Christmas!- A Summer campaign to encourage people to buy now or place items on layaway at amazing prices. It could be Black Friday or Christmas in July. Offer free turkeys with purchases of $300 or more.

50/50 Draw- Have customers enter their name to qualify. The qualifier flips a coin to see if they win Prize A or Prize B.

Demonstration Days- Host weekly seminars on how to use the product.

*More Random Sales Themes...*Welcome to Summer Sale (Spring, Fall, Winter), Improbable Prices, Utter Madness Sale, One Price Fits All, Lower Your Cost of Ownership, A World of Selection, Warehouse Sale, No Joke! The Savings are Real, Savings Fiasco, Minimum X% off Recommended Retail Prices, Shop Smart Sale, Manufacturer's Blow-Out Sale, Manufacturer's Un-Authorized Blow-Out Sale

__Brainstorming Notes.__

_____
_____
_____
_____
_____

Product Category Specific: IDEAS

Pawn Shop Cash Stash- This is an idea for a Pawn Shop but it could be used for any business. Just make your way to the Pawn Shop and gather 100 used CD's, games or movies. 99 of them have $1 inside. 1 case holds $100. Customers pick a case and receive the prize inside. Possibly, you could tie-in an 80s theme by going with 80s tunes and having 80s pricing. A lot of people love their 80s music! (Reminder. Make sure your target market loves 80s music and you aren't doing the theme because it's something you personally like.)

Mobile Repair Services: Appliances/Furnaces/Plumbing Ad Copy Idea- *'We don't waste time driving back and forth while you do without. We store twice as many parts in the truck as anyone else.'*

Furnace Service/Fireplace Repairs- Ad Slogan Idea. *'Give your furnace some love'* or *'Keep your fires burning inside.'*

Dead Sled Competition- *'Bring in the most beat-up, worst running, oldest snowmobile.'* Offer a Service discount to everyone who participates and a prize to the winner. Offer a minimum of $500 trade in value regardless of the condition of the sled.

Shoe Store Sale Ad Copy Idea- *'These shoes are made for selling.'*

Lawn and Garden Ad Copy Idea- Tree Sale. *'My bark is worse than my bite. I won't take a chunk out of your wallet'.*

Lawnmowers and other Lawn-Related Products- *'We're mowing down the prices.'*

Lighting and Bath Store- Miraculous Savings. *'Let there be light. Let there be bath accessories too.'*

Print Shop- Retro Business Image Rescue. *'Is your business image outdated? Do you have any image at all? Work with us to revive your logo and brand elements.'*

Jewellery/Jewelry Theme- *'A Sparkling Storewide Savings Event'.*

Brainstorming Notes.
_____
_____
_____
_____
_____

Pictures/Framing- 'Don't Fix 'em, Hide 'em' Sale. *'Don't fix holes and scratches in your wall, hide 'em instead.'*

Pizza/Sub- Tastes of the World (Month). Feature 5 International Recipes. Buy 4 and get the 5th free- Hawaiian, Italian, Mexican, Philly Beef, Thai Chicken. Once your Company Passport has 4 stamps, you get the 5th pizza/sub free.

Hot Tubs- 'Sup-ahhh Soothing Spa Sale'.

Mattresses Ad Copy Idea- *'Get a peaceful sleep and a great price that won't keep you up at night.'*

Mattresses Ad Copy Idea- Create an ad where a child jumps up and down on the bed. Mom hits ceiling because she has to get a new bed every 6 months...but not if she buys a quality brand from you.

Mattress Slogan Ideas- *'Get a good night's sleep starting tonight!'* or *'We'll put you to sleep, figuratively speaking, for a lot less.'* Or *'We're your King of Spring'*.

Gas Station- Free Gas Fridays. X# of customers get $10-$25 of free gas. Any business can host a Free Gas promotion by offering gas cards redeemable at the neighborhood gas station.

Bike Shop- World's Shortest Bike Race. Contestants race up a hill. How about the World's Fastest Bike Race? Race down the hill.

Ugliest or Oldest Bike- Bring your Ugliest or Oldest Bike in to get a discount on a new one. All participants are entered into a grand prize draw where 1 person will have their new bike purchase refunded.

Spa- The Day from Heck. Frustrated? Participants submit an entry form describing their day from heck. Simply writing it all out could be therapeutic in itself! The winner gets a weekend getaway and a spa treatment.

Spa- Queen for a Day. Send entries describing why you or a friend deserves to be treated like a Queen for a Day. The winner(s) gets the full treatment. All participants get a discount or bonus as a thank you for participating.

Brainstorming Notes.
_____
_____
_____
_____
_____

Restaurant- Diet Specials. Feature weight conscious meals at *'slimmer prices'*.

Search for the Ultimate Martini- Invite the public to submit their favourite recipe. Determine your finalists. Host a special celebration where you serve each finalist's Martini. Declare a winner through a taste testing challenge. You could have a judging committee or host a big party where everyone in attendance nominates their favourite before they leave. The winner's recipe goes on the menu.

Restaurant- Screaming Infants Night. New parents get a chance to go out where they won't be embarrassed. Host this on an off night and heavily promote it so you can give ample warning to anyone expecting a quiet night out. Have special offers, colouring books and don't forget the high chairs.

Diet- 1,000 Pound Challenge. Challenge your customers to lose 1,000 pounds collectively.

Fitness- On Site Aerobic Challenge. Host a contest for High Kicks, Jog-On-A-Spot and other aerobic moves.

Fitness- Quickie Lunch & Workout. Have special lunch hour rates for people without much time. Sell a light, healthy to-go lunch.

Coffee Sponsorship- 'Morning Show' Gourmet Coffee. Find a TV or Radio Station who will allow your coffee to be named the 'Official Coffee' of the show.

Gourmet Coffee- Host a weekly taste testing event. (Tasty Tuesdays?)

Donut Shop- The Donut Show. Have celebrities or media come in to make their own donut. Put it on the menu for a limited time. You can also show them baking 'live' through your social media channel.

Audio Equipment- Sound Trade Ins. Accept ancient audio video equipment in return for a discount on new equipment. Display the trade-ins for a few weeks because they make for good conversation pieces. Customers can re-live memories through a piece of equipment they once owned.

Brainstorming Notes.
_____
_____
_____
_____
_____

Video Equipment- Holiday Greetings. Customers record a holiday greeting from your location or while using your product. They submit their recordings via their social media account. Each video entered earns a discount and a contest entry.

Back to School Backpack- Win a backpack full of school stuff. This can be done anytime there's a return to school from a break or a holiday – it's not exclusive to late summer Back to School.

Grocery- Lettuce Make You Rich. Correctly guess how many heads of lettuce there are in the store to win cash and lottery tickets.

Furniture- Goodbye Wallflowers Blow-Out Sale. In stock merchandise that has been on the floor for over 6 months gets a clear-out price. Use a line like this in your ad: *'No one has asked to buy these wallflowers. Some are very attractive we think, but we have to find them new homes. They are on sale this weekend at 50% off.'*

Furniture- New Room Giveaway. Give away a bedroom set. Celebrate by having a sale where there's a discount on *'everything for the room'*.

Furniture- The Cash Couch. Qualify customers for a Lazy Sunday Promotion. 3 customers qualify. Each comes in and picks a couch. They get all the money hidden under the cushions. One couch holds the grand prize.

Furniture- A Couch Potato Ruined My Furniture. Enter via writing in/emailing in/submitting a social media post... Participants submit a story describing how their sofa was ruined by the resident Couch Potato. Everyone gets a discount. 1 grand prize winner is determined by a judging committee to make it even more fun. This could be quite humorous with good potential to go 'viral' because you'll hear very imaginative and entertaining stories.

Furniture- Assembly Competition. Host a competition to see who can assemble furniture the fastest. This works for Home Improvement stores also. Who can build the dog house the fastest?

Furniture- No Payments Event. This run-of-the-mill promotion becomes more interesting with a fun, creative angle...Guy says, *'great house - but where's the furniture?'* Friend says, *'Oh, it didn't come with furniture. The down payment killed my savings. Here, pull up a milk crate.'* Then the ad goes on to describe the No Payments Event and how you will rescue new home owners who are stretching their money as far as they can.

<u>Brainstorming Notes.</u>

_____
_____
_____
_____
_____

Heating- Free Gas for a Month. Incent new furnace purchasers by offering to pay for the 1st month's gas bill, *'after all, it can't be that much! Heck, we'll pay for 2 months!'* You can also take the angle where buyers can *'send your highest gas bill for a chance to get it paid by us'*.

Carpet- Free Cleaning with Purchase. Offer the free clean once a year for the first 2 years.

Carpet- Dinner is on Us. We send you out for dinner on the day we install your carpet.

Sports Store- Tough Guy/Girl. Host an endurance event. Contestants compete for most push-ups, sit-ups, etc., to win a significant prize…and bragging rights, of course.

Appliances (Dryer) Ad Copy Idea – *'Don't wear wet clothes in (insert your region's wet month), get a new dryer'*.

Locksmith- Summer Safety for Seniors. Show you care when you advertise safety tips, plus a senior's discount on the installation of new locks.

Greenhouses (or Home Improvement Stores)- Happy Hour. *'Are you thinking about all the yard work you have to do when you get home? Stop here before 6pm and receive 20% off your (insert supplies)'*.

Banks- Free Roses with new account openings *'for love of money'*.

Home Improvement- Q and A Sessions. Invite do-it-yourselfers to come and ask a few questions about particular projects. No selling. Offer coupons though. Focus on educating and building loyalty.

Decorating Dreams Contest Ad Copy Idea- Spouses debate about the décor. Who do you think wins this argument?

Pet Store- Halloween becomes Dog-o-Ween.

Pet Stores- Look-Alike Contest. Host a pet and owner look-alike contest. Nominate yourself or someone else – with their permission, we hope ☺.

Caterers- Open House. Cook up a spread for the event planners in the family. (Weddings, Showers, Birthdays, etc.). Invite people to stop by for samples, catering packages and to discuss ideas.

__Brainstorming Notes.__

_____
_____
_____
_____
_____

Garden Ponds- Product Demonstrations. How to set up and properly use a backyard pond.

Florist Ideas- Dog House Specials. It's pretty easy to come up with creative ads for this theme. There are likely a few real-life situations that make for very entertaining commercials. **Flower Power** *'a single rose can change your world.'* **Florist Temperature Outlook** for Saturday *'there's a possibility of a shower with cooler temperatures. To avoid this cold front...come to XYZ Flower Company ...The outlook can be very hot.'* **Ad Copy Idea**- *Charlie has four girlfriends. He needs flowers for a Happy Birthday, I Love You, a Just Because, and an 'I'm Sorry' because #4 found out about the others. Now, Charlie needs a 'Get Well' card.*

Florist- Name That Flower. Customers guess what kind of flower it is by its fragrance. Get a free one if you guess correctly. (Try to make it easy on them by making it multiple choice. You want them to get it right. You want this bonus flower included in the bouquet because they'll be excited to tell the story of how they won it.)

Florist- Host a simple contest. Customers are asked to *'Guess the number of flowers in this...'*.

Funeral Home Ad Copy Idea- Your actors are a couple who have been together for a long time. A Pre-Planning ad begins with *'Janice and I have always made important decisions together'*.

Duct Cleaning Ad Copy Idea- Stop the Meter Monster. Air conditioners and furnaces will work more efficiently with a cleaning. *'Make a healthy stop at (insert your business) and stop the meter monster.'*

Roofing Ad Copy Idea- Buddy gives an umbrella as a gift to his friend who is fixing his own roof. He tells him *'You should've called (insert your roofing company)'*.

Insurance- Catastrophe Call Series. Create a series of ads featuring 'insurance' situations. *'You'll never guess who I ran into... He's okay, not much damage. The car, on the other hand...It's a good thing I'm with ABC Insurance Company.'*

Kitchen Cabinets Ad Copy Idea- *'Get everything you need to give your ratty old kitchen cabinets a modern new look.'*

<u>Brainstorming Notes.</u>

_____
_____
_____
_____
_____

Rural Store Anti-Big Box Ad Copy Idea- *'We're not a big box store. We don't have the long line-ups or awful service like you get in town.'*

Three Computer Store Sale Themes- 1) A Memorable Sale. Offer free memory upgrades.

2) Software Sale. 3) Target business owners with a **Small Business Owner Open House.**

Garage Doors- The Best Beat Up Door. Participants submit a photo of their ugly garage door and the story behind the damage. There could be some entertaining stories with this one!

Ice Cream Ad Copy Idea- *'It's Always a Special Day at...'* Make up a variety of excuses to have Ice Cream by creating special theme days such as *'Give an Ice Cream to a Friend Day'*.

Brainstorming Notes.
_____
_____
_____
_____
_____

Christmas

Banks/Financial- Christmas Vacation Loans. Offer a $2000 interest free loan and *'put a vacation for yourself under the tree'*.

Money Grows on Trees- Customers pick a card off the tree at the checkout. The card contains a gift card or a discount. Include a couple of 50% off cards to add some excitement...and maybe they will spend more to try to win more? Let's hope.

Most Original Decorations- Your customers will get in the spirit with this promotion. Set up a tree (or a wall) where customers can bring in their handmade decoration and show off their creativity. Have a 1st, 2nd and 3rd place winner. Keep this one interesting by showing off the latest entries on your social media accounts.

Pet Holiday Photo Contest- Customers submit photo entries for contests like the Funniest or Most Heart-Warming Pet Photos from the Holidays. Have customers bring their pics into the store or post them on your social media account. Pet (and Kids) promotions are always popular!

Best Home Outdoor Decorations- Customers submit a picture of their decorations. Possibly make this a public voting contest. Participants include their home addresses so you can add them to the Best Home Outdoor Decorations Map. Families who like to go on 'Christmas Lights' tours will use the map to plan their route. And since they are out driving around, make sure there's a coffee shop sponsor who can offer a coupon on the map.

Give Your Parents a Christmas Break- Submit a letter stating why your Mom or Dad deserves a break. The winner(s) gets a night out, dinner, concert tickets, etc.

Win the Mystery Gift- This sounds like fun. Wrap a gift and put it on display. Customers can win by submitting a guess. Make a draw from all the correct guesses. Ideally, you'll have customers searching the aisles to find similar sized boxes.

Unwrap the Savings- Customers receive a gift box loaded with discounts for immediate savings. Plus, include coupons that can be used during Boxing Week or into January.

Gift Rebate- Customers enter a draw to win back the cost of their entire purchase. Fill out a ballot. Keep your receipt though! You might need it!

Brainstorming Notes.
_____
_____
_____
_____
_____

Christmas Ad Copy Idea- *'Even Mr. Scrooge would like our prices.'*

Santa's Middle Name- Customers and kids try to guess Santa's middle name. Use this slogan in your ads: *'Santa's middle name may be John or Jane but our middle name is Christmas'*.

Santa's Helper Photo Keepsake (Adult Product)- Take a photo with Santa's helpers – attractive Elves (hire Male and Female models).

Win-A-Kids Shopping Spree- You can win a shopping spree for your child(ren). They can have all that they can carry, up to a certain dollar limit.

Guess How Many Lights- Guess how many lights there are on the tree to win a prize.

Show Us Your… (store name or logo)- Homeowners use your logo or business name in their decorations. Make a competition out of it such as a voting contest.

Car Dealer Christmas 'Keys Off the Tree'- Customers pick keys off the Christmas Tree. If the key starts the showroom car, they win a prize like a car starter or other accessories worth a few hundred dollars.

Holiday Horror Stories- Customers submit their Christmas horror story. Anonymously share the stories on your website or social media. Find a media partner who would share the stories with their audiences, too. This could make for interesting and entertaining content.

Citizen of the Year- Nominate someone who goes all out to take care of others. A plaque/certificate/trophy is awarded to the person who is deemed the winner. They also receive a prize. The nominator receives a prize as well. Consider a bonus for all nominees because you value their contributions to the community.

New Year Retro Prices- Everything is priced at last year's prices or less.

January Clearance – Holiday Holdovers. Your ad message talks about how the spirit of giving has hit you and now you want to pass along some super values. *'We are practically giving away the merchandise.'*

Brainstorming Notes.
_____
_____
_____
_____
_____

Match Our Wish List- Customers give you their store wish list. If their list matches yours, they win. The beauty of this promotion is your customers are describing what they want most from your store. This is invaluable data. Build your customer/product profile by asking the participants to share their age, gender and any other demographic information you would like to know. Now you know where the demand is, what to stock and which merchandise is most desired by whom.

Also, have the customers opt-in to receive an email if anything on their wish list goes on sale.

Brainstorming Notes.
_____
_____
_____
_____

Ensuring an Effective Ad: Your Pre-Advertising Worksheet

As you create your next advertising message, there are some things you should keep top-of-mind before you begin. You want your ads to be true to your brand, to speak 'with' your audience and to achieve your business objectives.

Complete this questionnaire and you'll have the foundation for all future advertising and marketing messages, online and offline.

From now on, your advertising will be more effective because your messages play on your customer's/client's/patient's favourite radio station WII.FM (What's in It for Me).

Also, you will stop wasting money on buying the wrong Media Advertising Packages because you'll be completely in tune with the media that serves your target market the best.

What do you do?

Or whatever you are selling, what does it do? Try to make it clear and simple.

What is your specialty?

What is the one thing people need you for the most?

What difference do you make?

What difference do you, or what you are selling, make for others?

Your Unique Selling Proposition (USP)

The one defining consumer benefit that sets you apart from all competitors. What do customers gain from your brand that is different than all the rest? What is your point of difference?

Your Market Position

What is your current market share or ranking compared to your competitors?

What kind of Stereotypes do you face?

How are you, the companies in your product category, or what you sell, generally perceived by the public?

Your Brand Objective(s)

How do you want your customers to feel about your brand/business?

What is the Objective of your next ad campaign?

What is the short-term, measurable goal you want to achieve from this advertising campaign?

Who is your primary target audience?

Identify your most common customers or target group. (Gender, age group, income level, lifestyle, attitudes, what they do for fun, what is important to them…anything else that's particular about the types of people you serve.)

Do you have any Market Research?

Do you have any stats, surveys or polls that tell you who your customers are, what they want and what their attitudes are?

Tone of your ads.

How do you want your target market to feel after hearing or seeing your advertisement?

CTA – Your Call-To-Action

What specific action do you want your target market to take after being exposed to your message?

Elements in every ad.

What needs to go in every ad? This could be address, slogan, special sound effects, phone number, website, etc.

What Are Your Best Local Media Options?

Understand your options. What do they read and watch in your market? Is the local radio station, TV, newspaper or any other print media important in your market? Where are people spending time in general?

Next, ask these same questions again but with your best customers in mind. Where are they spending their media time? Their social media time? Narrow your options to the preferences of your best customers, clients and prospects.

#1 Tip for Writing Ads.

The best ads feature and support one main message or outcome. They don't try to cram in a grocery list of information. Don't overwhelm people into tuning you out. Keep It Simple, Silly.

Here's my format for creating successful commercials: There are 5 main ingredients.

1. Open with a message that;

   a) either addresses a problem or provides a real benefit to your target market, and

   b) identifies who this message is for. You want your prospect to immediately say 'That's me! This message is for me'.

2. Provide the solution to the problem.

3. Make your offer.

4. Make a call-to-action.

5. Tell them how or where to get the offer.